CW00516542

This Book Belongs To

Printed in Great Britain
by Amazon

48510652R00071